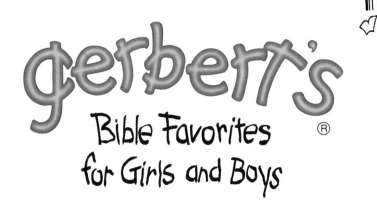

gerbert's
Bible Favorites
for Girls and Boys

®

Chariot Books™
David C. Cook Publishing Co.

VW

Chariot Books™ is an imprint of David C. Cook Publishing Co.
David C. Cook Publishing Co., Elgin, IL 60120
David C. Cook Publishing Co., Weston, Ontario
Nova Distribution, Ltd., Newton Abbot, England

GERBERT'S BIBLE FAVORITES FOR GIRLS AND BOYS
© 1992 by Home Sweet Home Educational Media Co. for text and photos.
© 1992 by David C. Cook for Bible illustrations.

Gerbert® is a registered trademark and exclusively administered by HSH Educational Media Co.

Excerpts taken from HSH's video text "Bible Blurberts One," written by Andy Holmes. Used by permission.

Edited by Jeannie Harmon
Cover and interior design by Elizabeth Thompson
Photography by Seth A. Smith
Bible illustrations by David Barnett and John Haysom

All Scripture quotations in this publication unless otherwise noted are from the *Holy Bible, New International Version.* Copyright © 1973, 1978, 1984, International Bible Society. Used by permission of Zondervan Bible Publishers.
First printing, 1992
Printed in United States of America
97 96 95 94 93 92 5 4 3 2 1

I just love the Bible, don't you? It has so many great stories!

Library of Congress Cataloging-in-Publication Data

Gerbert's Bible favorites for girls and boys / [edited by Jeannie Harmon].
    p.   cm.
    Summary: Presents retellings of more than a dozen familiar Old and New Testament stories, each accompanied by a brief introduction, discussion questions, and related Bible verses.
    ISBN 0-7814-0934-9
    1. Bible stories, English.   2. Children—Religious life. [1. Bible stories.]   I. Harmon, Jeannie.   II. Title.
BS551.2.G465   1992
220.9'505—dc20
                                               92-14580
                                                    CIP
                                                    AC

Table of Contents

Have you ever wanted to **HIDE**?

Have you ever thought that if you hid good enough and long enough, everything would be OK and you wouldn't have to tell anybody that something was wrong? Well, I've thought that too. Do you know the first people who lived thought the same thing? That's right.

I want to tell you a story about Adam and Eve and how the hateful, untruthful serpent tried to trick them into believing a lie. The story is in the Bible in the book called Genesis, and this is how it went. . . .

. . . .

Adam and Eve Disobey God

Genesis 1–3

Twinkle, twinkle, little star!

In the beginning, God created the whole world. He made the sun and He made the moon. He made all of the stars and knows every star by name. He made the birds, the fish, every kind of animal and every kind of tree and plant. He made everything, and then He made a man named Adam.

One day God planted a very beautiful garden with every tree that was pretty to look at and good for food. But there was one tree that Adam could not eat from. God told Adam, "You are free to eat from any tree in the garden; but you must not eat from the tree of the knowledge of good and evil, for when you eat of it you will surely die."

Then God said, "It is not good that man should be alone. I will make a helper suitable for him." So God made a woman called Eve. Adam and Eve were the first husband and wife ever to live. They were very happy in the beautiful garden God had made just for them.

Then one day the serpent began talking to Eve. He wanted Eve to disobey God. He told her if she would just eat of the tree of the knowledge of good and evil, she would become as smart as God. The serpent was very tricky with his words. So Eve took some fruit off the tree and ate it. Then she gave some to Adam and he ate it too.

Immediately they felt ashamed to see each other the way they had seen each other before. So they took leaves and covered up their bodies because they were embarrassed to be naked.

They heard the sound of God walking in the garden in the cool of the day and they were afraid because they had disobeyed Him. They hid among the trees.

The Lord called to Adam, "Where are you?"

Adam said, "I heard you coming so I hid. I wasn't wearing any clothes."

Then God asked, "Who told you that you were naked? Have you eaten from the tree?"

Adam was scared to tell God what he did, so he blamed it on Eve. "The woman you put here with me—she gave me some fruit from the tree, and I ate it."

Eve, Eve!
Where are you?

God was sad that Adam had not been completely truthful.

Then He asked Eve, "What is this you have done?"

But Eve was scared, too. She blamed it on the serpent. She said, "The serpent tricked me, and I ate the fruit."

Because Adam and Eve had believed the serpent's words, they could not be as free and happy as they were in the garden with God. Disobedience brought them much sorrow. But even though they disobeyed God, He still loved them and promised a much greater sacrifice to cover the sins of all men forever—Jesus Christ, our Lord and Savior.

. . . .

Let's talk about
HIDING:

You know what? . . .

When we do wrong we want to hide,
but joy comes when we're true.
So God sent Jesus from on high
to live in me and you.
So don't be afraid to tell the truth,
No matter how hard it may seem.
'Cause hiding will only keep you scared
But the truth will set you free.

That's right. So always tell the truth.

What do you think?

• Do you like to hide? When is hiding fun?

• Do you sometimes hide when you've done something wrong?

• What can you do when you do something wrong but don't mean to do it?

• • • • • • • • • • • • • • • • •

Teach me your way, O Lord, and
I will walk in your truth.
Psalm 86:11

God wants us to be honest and not **LIE** to each other.

He doesn't want us to trick other people or cheat them out of something. God wants us to tell the truth.

I want to tell you a story from the Bible about a man who was tricked by one of his closest friends. His name was Samson. This is how it happened. . . .

· ·

Samson Is Tricked by a Friend

Judges 13–16

A long time ago there lived a man named Samson. He was the strongest man that ever lived. Even before he was born, an angel told his mother that Samson would be a Nazirite and be dedicated to the Lord all of his life. Samson was never to cut his hair, eat grapes, or drink grape juice because a Nazirite couldn't do these things.

The spirit of the Lord came upon Samson many times and made him strong. One time as a young man, Samson killed a lion with his bare hands. Samson didn't have a weapon to fight the lion. He had only his hands.

"My strength comes from the Lord," he would boast.

He was so strong that everyone in the land of the Philistines was frightened of him and wanted to find out the secret of his strength.

"I'm not going to tell them," Samson said. "They will hurt me and mock God."

Then one day Samson fell in love with a woman named Delilah. When the leaders of the Philistines heard that Samson loved Delilah, they secretly visited her. "We will give you many pieces of silver if you find out the secret of Samson's strength," they told her.

So Delilah went to Samson and said, "Please tell me the secret of your strength. How can you be made weak?"

But Samson would only tease her. "If you tie me with new thongs or new ropes, I'll become as weak as any other man."

My strength comes
from the Lord.

13

So Delilah tied Samson with seven fresh thongs and then later with new ropes, and each time Samson broke them easily. He never told her the true secret of his strength. She kept asking him and asking him, day after day.

"Oh, Samson, if you loved me, you would tell me the secret of your strength," she would beg.

Samson was so irritated that he finally told her everything.

"If you shave my head, my strength will leave me."

That very night while Samson was asleep, Delilah had his hair cut so that he would be weak.

Then she called to him, "Samson, Samson, the Philistines are upon you!"

When Samson awoke, he was too weak to keep the Philistines from hurting him. His strength had left him. Samson was very sad.

• •

Let's talk about
LYING:

God is so great and He loves us so much! He gave us His Word, the Bible, to help us know how to treat others. His Word tells us that we should be honest and show love to our friends, not tell them lies (like Delilah did to Samson). True friends help each other at all times.

I'm very sad.

What do you think?

- Have you ever told a lie?

- How did you feel when you told a lie?

- What can you do to make things right with God when you lie?

• • • • • • • • • • • • • • • • • • • •

The Lord detests lying lips, but he delights in men who are truthful.
Proverbs 12:22

Have you ever had to be **BRAVE**?

Sometimes it isn't very easy, is it? It sure is good to know that God is always with me and always helping me. It makes it a lot easier to be brave. It sure does.

I want to tell you a story from the Bible about a young boy named David who was brave because he knew God was with him.

• •

David Fights a Giant

I Samuel 17

David was a shepherd. He watched his father's sheep and kept them safe from lions and bears. His older brothers were soldiers in the army of God's people. They went to fight the mighty Philistine army.

One day David's father told him, "Take some food to your brothers."

But when David found his brothers, they weren't fighting the enemy. All of the soldiers were afraid!

"What is the matter?" David asked.

"You'll see," his brothers said.

Soon a big enemy soldier walked out. He was a giant

Have you ever felt **SAD**?

One time I thought everyone had forgotten my birthday and I felt sad. God knows what it feels like to be sad. He really does! God is so kind and loving that when we're sad, He sees every tear and wants to tenderly wipe them dry. That right!

I'll explain what I mean by telling you a true story from the Bible about a time when David was sad.

. . . .

David Asks God for Help

I Samuel 30:1-20

David and his men came back from battle. It was a long trip, and they were very tired.

"Look!" a soldier shouted suddenly. "There's smoke coming from our town!"

When I'm sad, I put my trust in You, dear Lord.

named Goliath. "I want a man to fight me!" he shouted to the army of God's people. But none of the soldiers moved.

David said to the soldiers, "We should not be afraid of this giant. God is on our side. He will help us."

King Saul heard about the brave young man. He sent for David. "You are just a boy," King Saul said.

"I will fight the giant," David said. "God helped me kill a lion and a bear. I know He will help me kill this giant."

David picked up five stones for his sling. Then he went out to meet Goliath. The giant had a sword and a spear.

Goliath laughed when he saw David. "You are just a boy!" said Goliath.

I'll fight the giant!

David said, "You are brave because of your sword and spear. But I am brave because I trust God."

David put a stone in his sling. He pulled back the sling and let it go. The stone flew out of the sling and hit the giant in the head. Goliath fell down dead.

Then the soldiers chased away the Philistines. David had shown them how to be brave. He trusted God to help him.

. . . .

Let's talk about
BRAVERY:

I just love the Bible, don't. you? It has so many wonderful stories that let me know that God is always here to help me.

Sometimes at bedtime when Mommy or Daddy turns off the light, I feel alone and afraid. I think about David and how God helped him be brave, then I'm not afraid anymore. God is right here

in my bedroom with me. And when I go to the dentist and have to sit in that big chair, God is there, too. And when I go to get my hair cut, God is there, too. Everywhere I go, God is always with me, helping me to be brave. Yes, He is!

What a great God! I love Him, don't you?

The Lord is my helper; I will not be afraid.
Hebrews 13:6

What do y
think?

- What makes yc
afraid?

- What can you
remember that
always there t

. . . . .

When they reached Ziklag, they found that their enemies had burned the town and taken their families. Everything and everybody was gone—wives, children, animals—everything! David and his men cried and cried. They cried until they had no more tears.

"It's all David's fault!" the soldiers shouted. The men became so angry at David, they wanted to kill him!

David didn't know what to do next, so he asked God for help. "Dear Lord, please help me," David prayed. "We're so discouraged and sad! Should we go after our enemies?"

"Go. I will help you," God said.

So David and his men went after the enemy. On the way they found a man who had been left behind.

"Help! Help me, please!" the man cried weakly. David and his soldiers gave him food and water.

"Who are you?" David asked. "Where are you from?"

"I am a servant," the man answered. "I was left behind by the others. My people attacked your town and burned it."

"Can you take us to our enemies?" David asked.

Cast all your anxiety on him because
he cares for you.
I Peter 5:7

The man said, "Promise that you'll protect me, and I will take you to them." David agreed.

The servant took David and his men to the enemy camp. When they got there, everyone was eating and drinking and celebrating because they had captured David's town. They weren't paying any attention to those who were sneaking up on them!

David and his soldiers attacked. They fought their enemy all night and all the next day. And they won!

"We're saved!" the women and children cried.

Everyone laughed and cried and hugged each other. David thanked God for helping him when he was sad.

What do you think?

- Have you ever felt sad?

- What makes you feel sad?

- What can you do to feel better when you are sad?

Let's talk about SADNESS:

Have you felt sad today? Sometimes people say things that hurt your feelings and you feel sad. Sometimes things don't work out the way you want them to—like when you didn't get to go to the park because it rained, and you felt sad and disappointed.

Did you know that God knows what it's like to be disappointed and sad? Yes, He does. He understands when you hurt inside and when you cry, and it makes Him sad, too. He loves you very much and He cares about how you feel.

Hi! You know what? the Bible says a righteous man **SINGS** and rejoices.

So singing is pretty important stuff. I just love to sing myself. I like to sing when I walk and when I'm riding my bike, or when I'm just sitting in a chair. Sometimes I sing new songs; sometimes I sing songs you and I both know.

Well, let me tell you a story from the Bible about one time when singing was very important. The king over the whole land of Judah—his name was Jehoshaphat—was in a lot of trouble. But God used singing to help the king out. The story goes like this. . . .

Jehoshaphat Wins by Singing

II Chronicles 20:1-26

One day messengers came to the king's palace with some news. "Oh, King!" they cried. "A big enemy army is heading this way. They plan to fight us."

The people were frightened. How could their small army ever protect them?

The king said, "Go and tell the people to meet me at the temple. We'll ask God to help us."

Everyone—men, women, girls, and boys—hurried to the temple as the king began to pray. "Dear God, a big army is coming to attack us. We don't have enough soldiers to fight them. Please help us!"

Then a priest announced, "God has told me to tell you not to be afraid. The battle is not yours, but God's. Go out tomorrow to meet them. You will not have to fight. God will take care of everything."

How surprised the people were! They didn't know how God would answer their prayer, but they believed God and trusted Him. "Thank You, God," they said. Then the Levites began to praise God for His promise to help them.

Early the next morning King Jehoshaphat called his army together. "Trust God," he told them. "He will answer our prayer."

Then King Jehoshaphat chose singers to march in front of the army. When everyone was in place, the king led them out to meet the enemy army.

As they marched along, the singers sang praises to God. "Give thanks to the Lord," they sang, "for His love lasts forever."

King Jehoshaphat, the singers, and the soldiers kept marching right to the top of the last hill. On the other side was the enemy camp. What a surprise they had when they reached the top—the enemy was dead! The soldiers had started to fight with one another, and now none of them was alive.

Come on, everybody! It's time to sing to the Lord!

By trusting God and singing praises to Him, King Jehoshaphat and his army didn't have to fight at all. God had won the battle for them!

· ·

Let's talk about
SINGING:

I love to sing. Sometimes when I feel sad inside, I start singing and my sadness goes away. Here's a song I like to sing:

Next time you feel like singing
And doing the tap-tap-tap,
Sing a song to make you strong
Like old Jehoshaphat.
Sing a song to Jesus.
Sing it loud and clear,
'Cause when you sing a song to God,
You know He's always near.

Tada! I just made that up! So remember always to sing.

What do you think?

- Is it hard to sing when you feel sad?

- When you sing, does it make you feel happy?

. . . .

Sing and make music in your heart to the Lord.
Ephesians 5:19

Remember,
always sing!

27

Have you ever been really excited about something, but you had to **WAIT** for it?

Maybe you had to wait to go to the circus or to open presents on your birthday. Oh, it's so hard to wait when it's something really good. But you know what? God's Word, the Bible, tells us that there's a right time for everything. Sometimes we have to be patient and wait for that special time when things will happen. I'll show you what I mean. . . .

• •

A Special Time for Everything

Ecclesiastes 3:1-7

There's a time to plant . . .
and a time to pick what is planted.

and a time to weep . . .

and a time to laugh . . .

and a time to mourn (that means be sad) . . .

and a time to dance.

There's a time to be silent (like when your baby brother or sister is sleeping) . . .

and there's a time to talk (like after you raise your hand and the teacher calls on you—that's the time to talk) . . .

For everything there is a season . . .
and a time for every matter under heaven.

Sometimes I like to dance!

Let's talk about
WAITING:

I guess it is my time to wait
and I will wait . . . with great
excitement!

What do you think?

- What day is special to you? (birthday, Christmas, etc.)

- What do you like best about that day?

- Do you know who gave you that special day to enjoy?

Trust in the Lord
with all your heart
and lean not on your
own understanding.
Proverbs 3:5

Have you ever felt **AFRAID**?

It's scary, isn't it? Sometimes when you're scared, you don't know what to do. Well, I want to tell you a story about a bunch of men who felt afraid. It's a story from the Bible and we know that if it's in the Bible, it's a true story. It really, really happened. This is how the story goes. . . .

Jesus and the Big Storm

Mark 4:35-41

One day Jesus was teaching people about God. He had talked to the people all day and He was very tired.

"You're so tired, Jesus," His disciples said. "You must rest."

"Yes," said Jesus. "Let's go across the lake."

So Jesus and His disciples got into a boat. It took a long time to sail across the big lake. Soon Jesus fell asleep.

While He slept, His disciples talked quietly together. The sky grew dark with storm clouds. The wind began to blow.

"Look how dark the sky is getting," said one. "I'm afraid it's going to storm before we reach the other side of the lake."

31

The wind began to blow harder and harder. The waves grew higher and higher. Thunder began to rumble. Then the rain came down, filling the boat with water. Everyone was afraid!

"We're going to drown!" cried one of the disciples.

"Look, Jesus is still sleeping!" another said.

"Wake up, Jesus! We're afraid! Don't You care if we sink?" the disciples shouted.

Jesus opened His eyes and looked around. He saw the dark sky overhead. He saw the great waves tossing the boat, and He heard the wind howling.

Jesus spoke to the wind and the waves.

Save us, Lord!
Save us!

"Quiet! Be still," said Jesus. Suddenly the wind stopped blowing. The waves stopped beating against the boat and the lake became as smooth as glass. The sky grew clear again.

Jesus said quietly, "Why were you so afraid? Didn't you know that I would keep you safe?"

The disciples looked at each other in great surprise.

"How wonderful Jesus is," they said. "Even the wind and the waves obey Him. We should never be afraid when He is with us."

Let's talk about
BEING AFRAID:

Did you know that Jesus is always with you? Yes, He is. He's invisible. He's sitting next to you right now. Can you believe it? Because He loves you so much, He doesn't want you to feel lonely or afraid, so He stays right beside you all the time. That's right. And when you feel alone or afraid, all you have to do is start talking to Him. He hears every word you say and He's ready to help you out. God is so great!

What do you think?

- Have you ever been so afraid that you didn't know what to do?

- Who is always watching over you?

- What can you do to feel better when you're afraid?

Do not be afraid, for I am with you.
Genesis 26:24

It's so hard to **DO THE RIGHT THING**. I really do love God and want to obey Him.

But sometimes I feel like doing what I want to do, whether it's right or not. You know what? There's a story in the Bible about a boy who had a pretty hard time choosing to do the right thing, too. You can find this story in your Bible in the book of Matthew, chapter 21, verses 28-31. . . .

· ·

The Son Who Kept His Promise

Matthew 21:28-31

One day Jesus told this story.

A man had a vineyard. He said to his first son, "Please pick grapes for me today."

But the son said, "No, I will not work. I have other things to do."

I'm going to play baseball today!

35

Then the father told his second son, "Please pick grapes for me today." The second son promised, "I'll be glad to work for you, Father"

Later the first son began to feel bad. He changed his mind and decided to work. "I should obey my father," he said. So he went and worked all day.

The second son also changed his mind. "I don't feel like working," he said. "I'll find something else to do." This son did not keep his promise.

Then Jesus asked the people with Him, "Which son did the right thing?"

The people answered, "The first son. The second son did not keep his promise."

I promised Mommy that I would pick up my toys.

Let's talk about
DOING THE RIGHT THING:

God wants you to keep the promises you make—like when you promise your mommy you'll pick up your toys. Sometimes it's very hard because you want to do something else instead.

But if you promise, God wants you to do what you promised to do. Otherwise, it's just like telling a lie. And God hates lies. God loves it when we choose to keep our word.

What do you think?

- Have you ever made a promise?

- What did you promise to do?

- Did you feel good when you kept your promise?

• • • • • • • • • • • • • • • • •

Whatever your lips utter you
must be sure to do.
Deuteronomy 23:23

You are my **FRIEND.**

Roary is my friend, too. Friends are wonderful. God likes it when we treat each other like friends.

Do you know that we can treat others as friends even if we don't know them? Yes, that's right. I want to tell you a story from the Bible about a man who was a friend to someone he didn't know. He was called the good Samaritan.

· ·

The Good Samaritan

Luke 10:30-37

Once there was a man who wanted to go to the city of Jericho. He traveled along a lonely road. Soon robbers jumped out and attacked him. They hit the man until he was almost dead. Then they took his money and clothes, and ran away.

The poor, hurt man lay by the side of the road, hoping that someone would help him. Soon he heard foot-steps. It was a priest from the temple. But the priest did not stop to help the man. Instead, he walked on down the road.

A little while later, the hurt man heard footsteps again. This time it was a Levite who served in the temple. But when the Levite saw the hurt man, he walked away, too.

"Won't anyone stop to help me?" cried the hurt man to himself.

Finally, a Samaritan man came down the road, riding his donkey.

"A Samaritan won't stop and help me," thought the hurt man sadly. "Samaritans don't like people from my country."

But the Samaritan saw the wounded man and felt sorry for him. He stopped and knelt down beside the man, looking at his wounds. The Samaritan washed the man's cuts and bruises and poured oil on them to help them feel better. When he finished, he lifted the hurt man onto his own donkey and took him to the city.

"Do you have a room for my friend?" the Samaritan asked the innkeeper. "He needs a comfortable bed for the night." So they put the hurt man in a bed and the Samaritan cared for him all night long.

In the morning, the Samaritan said, "Here is some money. Take good care of my friend while I am gone. If you need more money, I will pay you when I come back."

I wonder if I will find a friend to help today!

Let's talk about FRIENDS:

God wants us to help when we see someone in need. Maybe it's a new boy or girl at your school who feels lonely, or maybe a little friend you see at the park. You might be surprised how happy it can make someone feel when you smile at him or her and say, "Hello! How are you?" God likes it when we think about other people's feelings and treat them like we'd want them to treat us.

I'm sure you can think of lots of wonderful ways to treat others kindly. We can share our cookies or invite other kids to play with us. We can ride bikes together or let them play on our swings. Sometimes I say, "Hi! My name is Gerbert. I want to be your friend." And before long, I have a new friend.

Do to others as you would have them do to you.
Luke 6:31

What do you think?

- Do you have a friend?

- Why is he or she a good friend?

- What can you do to be a friend to someone?

41

Have you ever **LOST** something that was very special to you?

It's a terrible feeling, isn't it? I want to tell you about a man in the Bible who lost something that was special to him, and what he did about it. . . .

. . . .

The Lost Sheep

Luke 15:1-7

Once there was shepherd who had many sheep. He had more than one. He had more than ten. He had one hundred sheep!

The shepherd loved his sheep very much. Every morning he took the sheep to eat green grass. When it was almost dark, the shepherd brought the sheep back to the pen where they would be safe. Sometimes he would sing to them.

Every night the shepherd counted the sheep as they ran into the safe pen. He counted, "One, two, three, four, five, six. . . ." He kept counting until at last he was near the end. "Ninety-seven, ninety-eight, ninety-nine, one hundred. All of my sheep are safe."

Then one day as he counted, he noticed something strange. "Ninety-seven, ninety-eight, ninety-nine. . . . Ninety-nine? There should be one hundred sheep. One of my sheep is lost!" the shepherd said.

After he made sure the other sheep were safe, the

shepherd went to look for that one lost sheep. The sun
went down, and it was dark, but still the shepherd
looked. He looked behind bushes. He looked behind
big rocks. Then at last he heard a sound that made
him feel happy.

"Baa," said the sheep.

"There you are," the shepherd said as he took the
sheep into his arms. "I'm so glad I found you. I'm
going to tell all my friends that I found my lost sheep."

The shepherd carefully picked up the sheep and carried
him back home. Then he called his friends and neighbors and said, "Come to a party. I found my lost sheep.
Come and rejoice with me!"

Let's talk about
BEING LOST:

God loves you. Did you know that? Yes! And He loves me, too. God loves us and wants to take care of us. He is like the shepherd and we are like the sheep.

He wants everybody to be in His family. Boy, that would be a big family! God is happy when a person wants to be part of His family. God always says, "Yes." He never turns anyone away. Oh! It feels so-o-o-o-o good to be in the family of God!

What do you think?

• Have you ever lost anything?

• How did you feel?

• What could you do to help find what was lost?

We love because he first loved us.
I John 4:19

44

Have you ever gotten so frustrated that you wanted to **QUIT**?

I have. At first, I couldn't get my picture to look the way I wanted it to and I got kind of frustrated. But when I kept trying, the picture finally turned out good and I'm glad I didn't give up.

I want to tell you a story about a lady who lost one of her silver coins. She had to look for a long time, but she didn't give up. She finally found it.

• •

The Lost Coin

Luke 15:8-10

Once there was a woman who had ten silver coins. Count them . . . 1, 2, 3, 4, 5, 6, 7, 8, 9, 10!

But then she lost one of her coins and only had nine. Count again . . . 1, 2, 3, 4, 5, 6, 7, 8, 9, . . . 9? Where was the tenth coin?

She looked everywhere but couldn't find her lost coin. She looked around the table, by her chair, under her bed. Soon she got her lamp to brighten up the room. Now she would be able to see better and surely she would find her coin. But the extra light didn't help.

So she got her broom. She swept and swept. She swept under everything looking for her lost coin. Finally, she found her coin. She was so happy that she called all of her friends and neighbors and told them she had found her lost coin.

Let's talk about
QUITTING:

I don't know about you, but sometimes I get frustrated. When I was learning to tie my shoes, I would get the shoelaces all tangled up, and I'd get so frustrated that I wanted to quit! Then my Mommy would tell me, "Gerbert, be patient. You'll get those shoes tied all by yourself real soon."

I thought about what she said. And you know what? If I would have stopped when I felt like quitting, I never would have learned how to tie my shoes.

Sometimes I ask God to help me. I say, "God, You know that I am frustrated and want to quit. Please help me." And He always helps me get the job done.

"God, You know that I'm frustrated and want to quit. Please help me."

This lamp will help me find the lost coin.

What do you think?

- Have you ever felt that you couldn't do something, no matter how many times you've tried?

- How do you feel when you can finally do what you wanted to do?

- What is one thing you can do all by yourself?

Whatever you do, work at it with all your heart.
Colossians 3:23

Have you ever been really **HAPPY** about something?

Happiness is a wonderful thing, isn't it? I want to tell you a story from the Bible about a man who became very happy because of the kindness of Jesus. Here's how it happened. . . .

· ·

Jesus Heals a Blind Beggar

John 9:1-7

Once there was a man who was blind and poor. He was called a beggar because he begged for money or food. Everyday he would cry out to those who passed by him, "Alms! Alms for the poor!"

He had always been blind, from the moment he was born. Indeed his eyes had never seen a beautiful sunrise or a soothing sunset. He'd never even seen his own face or known the color of his hair. Until one day, one unforgettably special day. . . .

Jesus was walking with His disciples and they saw the poor blind man. Jesus said, "This blind man needs help. I will help him. You'll see what God's power can do."

Alms! Alms for
the poor!

Jesus went up to the blind man. He spat on the dirt and made a little bit of mud. Then He spread the mud on the eyes of the blind man. Jesus told him, "Go wash in the Pool of Siloam."

The blind man felt his way to the pool. He washed his face with the water and a miracle happened. The blind man was healed! He could see!

He hurried home with happy news to tell! His neighbors and all those who had seen him as a beggar said, "Isn't this the same man who used to sit and beg?"

"Yes, I am he," the man said. "Jesus put mud on my eyes and told me to go wash in the Pool of Siloam. So I did and now I can see. Jesus made me well!"

The once blind beggar was very happy. He knew that Jesus was the greatest man that ever lived—He was God come to earth.

Let's talk about
HAPPINESS:

I love feeling happy inside. Yes, I do. When I got my new bicycle, I was so happy, all I could do was grin. And you know what? When I was smiling, everyone around me smiled, too. (Snap! Just like that!)

God wants us to be happy knowing that He is always there to help us. If we have a problem, we can talk to Him and He'll help us find the answer. That's enough to make anybody happy.

I can see! I can see!
Jesus made me well!

What do you think?

- What makes you feel very happy?

- Do you know that God wants you to feel happy inside?

- When you are happy, how does your face look?

Ask and it will be given to you; seek
and you will find.
Luke 11:9

51

Have you ever tried to save up **MONEY**?

Maybe you're saving up money right now to buy something special. I put nickels and dimes that I'm saving in a piggy bank.

I want to tell you a story from the Bible about a lady who had some coins, but she didn't put them in a piggy bank. Here's what she did. . . .

. . . .

A Widow Gives Her Offering

Mark 12:41-44

One day when Jesus had finished teaching in the temple, He sat down near the offering box. Some of His disciples were there too. They watched as people gave their offerings to God.

The people dropped their money into the box as they entered the temple. There was no paper money, only coins. *Plink*! went the little coins. *Clunk*! went the big coins. Everyone heard the noise the coins made. While Jesus sat watching, a rich man walked by to drop in his offering. He carried a money bag made of beautiful leather. The bag was full of money. He put his hand into the money bag and took out some gold coins. One at a time, he let the big gold coins fall into the offering box. *Clunk, clunk, clunk*!

Give, and it will be given to you.
Luke 6:38

I want everyone to
see my offering.

What do you think?

- Did you ever give up something that you really wanted to keep?

- Is it easier to give away things you don't really like?

- When somebody likes what you've given him or her, how does it make you feel inside?

• • • • • • • • • • • • • • • • •

The rich man looked around to see how many people were watching. He was glad his money made so much noise. He wanted everyone to know that he had given a big offering.

Jesus saw many people come and go. They all put money in the offering box. Big coins, small coins. Loud coins, soft coins. Many of them did not think about giving the money to God. They only thought about what other people would think of them.

Then a widow came into the temple. Her husband had died and she didn't have much money. She dropped two small coins into the box. *Plink, plink!* She knew it did not sound like much money. But she loved God and wanted to give Him an offering.

Jesus told His disciples to look at her. "Many rich people have come here," He said. "They put in a little of their money. But this woman gave God her best. She gave Him everything she had."

• •

Let's talk about **MONEY**:

You know what? Being wise with our money is very important. Sometimes our money (or the things that we buy with our money) becomes more important to us than God. We get selfish and don't want to share with others. God likes it when we love Him *more* than we love money or things. When we love God, we want to share what we have with other people.

Have you ever felt **DISAPPOINTED**?

There was this guy in the Bible named Peter who felt disappointed. I learned about him in Sunday school. I like stories from the Bible because they are about people like you and me—people who laughed and cried, hoped and dreamed. God loved them all, just like He loves you and me. That's right.

• •

Peter Denies His Friend

Mark 1:16-18; 14

A long time ago there lived a man named Peter. Peter was a fisherman. Every day he and his brother, Andrew, would get into their boat and go out fishing. But all those days of fishing came to an end the day the Lord Jesus said, "Come follow Me and I'll make you fish for men."

Peter decided right then that he wanted to follow Jesus so he got up and followed Him.

Then one day Peter and the other disciples were eating a very special supper with Jesus. He told them that He was going to leave them soon and go to His father's house in heaven. Jesus told them that many terrible things were going to happen to Him and that all of them would get scared and run away and hide. But Peter said, "Not me, Lord. I will not run away. I'll go anywhere with You and I'll do anything for You."

Jesus said to Peter, "Before the rooster crows twice, you will say you don't know Me three times."

Peter could not believe that he would ever do such a thing. He loved Jesus so much. But later that same night everything Jesus said came true! Soldiers came and arrested Jesus, and all the other disciples ran away. But Peter followed and waited in the courtyard.

A maid saw Peter and said, "This man was with Jesus." Peter lied and said, "I don't know Him." He hoped no one else would recognize him. He didn't want to get arrested too!

Then a little later she said to Peter again, "You're one of Jesus' disciples."

"No, I'm not." Peter lied again.

Then someone else said, "I'm sure you're one of His disciples."

Again Peter said, "I don't know Jesus. I don't know Him."

Immediately the rooster crowed and Peter remembered what Jesus had said. Peter was very sad. He went away and cried for a long time because he felt so ashamed. He was disappointed that he had denied knowing Jesus.

But after the Lord Jesus came back to life, Peter had the chance to talk to Jesus and tell Him that he loved Him. Jesus didn't get mad at Peter or scold him. Instead, Jesus made him feel better, and He let Peter know that He loved him very much.

● ●

Let's talk about
DISAPPOINTMENT:

Sometimes we do things that hurt other people. Maybe we say something that isn't true or laugh at someone because he is different from us. Then later we feel sad because of the way we treated that person. We are disappointed, not because we didn't get something, but because we did something wrong and are now sorry about it. God is so loving that He tells us in His Word that we can go to that person and say, "I'm sorry. Forgive me for what I did." And you know what? Once we say we're sorry, we help the hurt in his or her heart to heal, and we all feel better about ourselves. Wow! God is so smart!

What do you think?

- Do you ever say bad things about someone?

- What can we say to let that person know we are sorry?

- What can we tell someone to make him or her feel loved?

As I have loved you, so you must love one another. By this all men will know that you are my disciples.
John 13:34

Yes, Lord, I love You,
I love You, I love You.

Have you ever received a **GIFT**?

It's pretty exciting, isn't it? It can really make you feel special and happy. I want to tell you about a lady who loved to make people feel special. Her name was Dorcas and you can read about her in the Bible. The Bible is the best book ever.

Dorcas Helps Others

Acts 9:36-43

Dorcas lived in the city of Joppa. Dorcas did many kind things for other people. She often made clothes, then gave them away to people who really needed them. Everyone loved Dorcas.

One day Dorcas got sick. She was very, very sick. Her friends tried to help, but there was nothing they could do. Before long, she died. Everyone was sad.

"What will we do without Dorcas?" they said to each other.

Then someone got an idea. "Peter is not far away," he said. "God helps him heal people who are sick."

Dorcas's friends got excited. "Let's get Peter," they said.

Two men went to find Peter. When they found him, they told him the sad news. "Please come right away,"

they said to Peter. "Our friend Dorcas was sick and now she has died."

Peter went with them. He decided he had better check things out to see if he could help Dorcas. Soon they got to Joppa.

Many people were at Dorcas's house. They were sad because their friend was dead. They were crying.

"Look at these clothes," they told Peter. "Dorcas made them for us."

Peter looked at all the things that Dorcas had made for the people. Then he asked them to go outside. He got on his knees and prayed to God.

Then Peter said, "Get up, Dorcas."

Dorcas opened her eyes and sat up. Peter took Dorcas's hand and helped her get up. Then he called her friends. Were they surprised!

"Dorcas is alive! Dorcas is alive!" they shouted as they ran to hug her.

All over Joppa the news spread that Dorcas had been raised from the dead. Many people believed in Jesus because Peter helped their friend Dorcas.

• •

Let's talk about
GIVING:

God is so neat, isn't He?

The Bible says that you and I are God's special creations, and that we were created to do good works for His glory.

Doing a good work for someone is like giving that person a beautiful gift. Dorcas did a good work when she made clothes for people who didn't have any clothes to wear.

You and I can do lots of things to help others. We can help Mommy carry in the groceries or help Daddy wash the car. We can pick up our toys or help pass out cookies in Sunday school. Whenever we do kind things for others, we give of ourselves. This makes God smile from ear to ear!

What do you think?

- What can you do to help someone?

- How does it feel when someone does something nice for you?

- How does God feel when we help others?

Each one should use whatever gift he has received to serve others.
I Peter 4:10

When you help Daddy wash the car, what a beautiful gift you are!